EMBELLISHED NOTIONS

Shadows and Light

SYED OMER

Preface

Have you ever felt lost and alone, wondering if there's any hope left in the world? Have you ever had strange and unsettling thoughts that you couldn't quite put into words? That's where I was when I started writing this book.

For a long time, I kept a record of my thoughts and emotions, not sure what to do with them. But then I realized that these words had the power to touch others who might be going through similar struggles. So, I turned my thoughts into poetry, hoping to express the full range of my feelings and experiences.

Through my writing, I explore the highs and lows of life, the moments of joy and pain that shape us into who we are. I share my own experiences, as well as observations of others, in the hope that my words might resonate with someone else who needs a little bit of hope and inspiration.

This book is a reflection of my journey, a record of the emotions and experiences that have shaped me. I hope that it will help you to connect with your own feelings and experiences, and to find comfort and hope in the midst of life's struggle.

Perception Index

1. Hope

When life feels like a steep slope,

And your efforts don't seem to bring any
hope,

When you can't find the joy that you seek,

And everything you once loved now seems
bleak,

When you feel lost and disconnected,

And the graph of your life is falling,
unaffected,

It's easy to give in and let go,

To believe that there's nothing more to
grow.

But hold on, my friend, don't lose your
grip,

For there's something that can help you
rip,

Through the darkness and the pain,

And bring the sunshine back again.

It's hope, the ever-shining light,

That keeps you going through the darkest
night,

The faith that things will get better,

And the belief that you'll come out
stronger.

Hope is the flame that never dies,

That helps you reach for the skies,

And turn your life's graph upwards,

Towards a future that's bright and
glorious.

So hold onto hope with all your might,

And let it guide you through the night,

For when you keep your faith alive,

You'll find the strength to survive.

2. Who is truly a man of love?

A man of love is one who's kind,
Compassionate and loving, with an open mind,
He responds with love to life's ups and downs,
And spreads kindness and joy wherever he's found.

If you comfort him with love and care,
He'll return it back like a child so rare,
But if you hurt him with hate and disdain,
He'll seek peace and love, and not return the same.

For a man of love knows hate only breeds,
More of the same, and that's not what he needs,
He chooses to love, no matter the cost,
And in doing so, gains more than he's lost.

 And let kindness and
compassion never end,
For it's in loving that we
truly find,
The peace and joy that
heal the mind.

3. Dilemma

I am like a barren desert in a land of rainfall,

A lonely expanse where the sun beats down
on me, unbearably tall.

But when the clouds come rolling in,

A sense of euphoria sweeps over me, and
hope begins.

I can feel the moisture in the air,

The scent of petrichor fills me with a sense of
repair.

And as the clouds
grow pregnant with
rain,

I can almost taste
the coolness on my
parched terrain.

But then, as the raindrops begin to fall,

I am left wanting, as if it's mocking my call.

The drops that touch my skin,

Are but a mere tease, and a fleeting whim.

For I know that it won't last long,

That I'll once again be left in the sun, longing.

I can't help but wonder why,

The clouds continue to toy with my feelings,
leaving me high and dry.

Perhaps it's because they take pity on me,

For they know I am like a desert, barren and
empty.

But then again, maybe it's not love they feel,

Perhaps it's just a game they play, something
unreal.

And yet, even in the midst of my confusion,

I find myself drawn to the cool breeze, a
sweet infusion.

For even if the rain doesn't come,

The breeze brings with it a sense of peace, a
soothing hum.

So maybe it's not about the rain at all,

Maybe it's the cool breeze that I crave, its
gentle call.

For in its presence, I feel alive,

And all my worries and doubts begin to
subside.

In the end, I'm left feeling uncertain,

Wondering if the clouds' love is genuine or a
mere distraction.

But one thing's for sure, in the midst of it all,

I'll keep searching for the cool breeze, and its
sweet, gentle call.

4. Expensive Things

This is a feeling we all know,
Greeting our loved one's day and night.
It is a mellow in our mouths flowing out of
the lips,
As soon as they come into our sight.

Never asked in return,
Love or the greeting you've given.
But in the darkest of times,
We get something in return.

For the millions of your good mornings,
Good afternoons and evenings.
You earn the most expensive,
The sweetest of goodbyes.

5. A Paragon Rendezvous

When we meet,

I wish,

If there was a twilight,

If time paused,

If there was a relaxing breeze,

If birds learnt love from us,

If the piano itself played a

romanticised music.

Everything else obeying the

paradigm and it went on and

on and on,

But both of us?

6. Broken Times

The hands of my clock of life are broken.

The clock has gone weary.

Without the hands,

I do not know the time.

Maybe,

That is the reason

It's been years,

Yet

I'm living the same day where I was with you.

7. The Chase

In constant pursuit, we ran

Following in each other's footsteps.

Never did we pause or rest.

You chased after love,

While I chased after you.

But little did you realize,

Love was behind me, too.

It caught hold of me and stayed,

While you forged an alliance with hate.

But little did you know,

Hate is always trailed by evil.

Now you must confront it all,

While I, with love's help, stand tall.

8. Inevitable

Love doesn't tell us it just happens.
And when it does it leaves us startling.

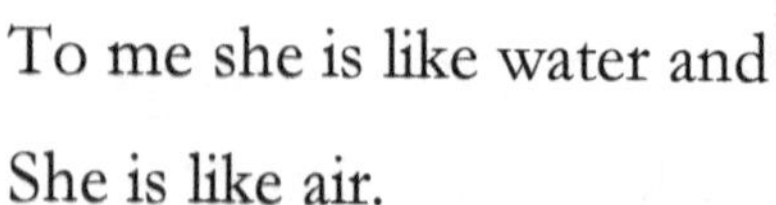

But in my heart,
She was and she will
Always be there.

To me she is like water and
She is like air.

But some ask me,
"if you loved her,
Why didn't you tell her
And why didn't you dare?"

She was in love with someone else
And the time was unfair.

Again, they ask me,

"Do you still love her?"

I don't know about love

What I always did

And I always will is care.

9. The Devil Has Us All

We don't know yet,

But we are all possessed.

Somethings there are that can't be professed

So Look around you,

Everything is on the verge to fall.

Why don't we get it?

This is his new kind of Maul.

Just, look around you again,

There are disciples of his, standing tall.

While, the good ones seem to brutally fall.

The kingdom of the devil is about to begin,

As we humans become empty from within.

So, look around you again,

The tender minds of the teens being spoiled.

Evasive and evil thoughts piled.

We are all left on the side of dark.

So, on the journey the devil can embark.

Look around you again,

Just in the name of equality genders being
changed.

Being Taught we are,

Men to be weak,

Women have nothing to be ashamed.

Yes, we are all possessed.

Because we've forgotten the teachings of the
truthful ones who exclaimed.

Look around you again,

The devil has us all.

"Humanity, shield yourself from the devil and
run away towards God."

Same they did say,

Muhammad, Ram and Paul.

Do it,

A few steps necessary to recede,

And to let your lord lead.

Close your eyes and once to him you call.

Or be sure to be doomed.

And bear with the truth,

That the-

The devil has us all.

10. Spring Has Begun

Spring has begun,

So, look at the bright sun.

My favourite flower,

Has blossomed and it's a wonder.

And it feels awesome,

To see it in full bloom.

The seeds of this flower that fell into my heart
long ago,

Are now being cherished, and it's like a dream
come true.

With the perfect amount of love,

I think it's a good start, and it's beautiful to
see them grow.

The air of your smile,

That shakes my plants off.

And spread the seeds aloft.

Let the smile continue,

And the strength of our love's sinew.

This is my wish,

My lovely flower.

We need to spread the seeds,

And increase the reign of our love flowers,

Because every time the spring comes,

Summer too is away just a few hours.

11. I'm A Loner

I'm a loner,

The rent payer and the owner.

Alone I have come and alone I'll go,

Because I do, I know,

That only in loneliness I grow.

Attention of people isn't something I want to
Ace,

All I seek for is my little space.

How much you try to fathom,

You will not me not know me more than that
of an atom.

From the start moon hath been my friend,

It will remain the same until my end.

Do not worry about me because,

I'm a loner,

The rent payer and the owner.

12. In Secret

In secret, we have met,

In silence, we have smiled,

For speaking with our mouths is not an
option yet.

But oh, my eyes, they can hear,

And your eyes, they just have to speak,

And in that silent exchange, our love is clear.

No words need to be spoken, no sounds need
to be made,

For the language of the eyes is a symphony
that needs no aid.

So let us continue to meet in secret,

And smile in silence, our love to keep it.

13. The Ripple

The ethereal beauty of the aurora danced across the sky, casting a luminous glow upon the stillness of the night. The magnificence of nature was in full display, and I felt a sense of awe and reverence in the presence of such a grand spectacle.

As I stood there, transfixed by the otherworldly scene before me, I couldn't help but feel a sense of nostalgia wash over me. Memories of a distant past, long forgotten, began to resurface, their tendrils slowly creeping into my consciousness like a thick fog.

I felt a pang of melancholy, a longing for a time that had passed, and a yearning for something that I could not quite grasp. It was as if I were searching for a missing piece of myself, a fragment of my soul that had been lost to the mists of time.

And yet, as I gazed upon the majestic display
of the aurora, I felt a glimmer of hope ignite
within me. It was a feeling of renewal, a sense
of rebirth that brought with it a newfound
clarity and purpose.

In that moment, I realized that life, like the
aurora, was a magnificent display of light and
colour, a tapestry of experiences that weaved
together to create a beautiful and unique
story. And though the memories of the past
may linger, they serve only to guide us
forward, towards a future that is bright and
full of promise.

So, I stood there, basking in the radiance of
the aurora, my heart full of wonder and
gratitude for the beauty of the world and the
journey that lay ahead.

14. Alzheimer's

I am so much engaged in love,

That I oft forget that she doesn't love me back.

I am so much engaged in my thoughts,

That I oft forget that she doesn't even think about me.

I am so much engaged in reminiscing,

That I oft forget that she doesn't even remember me.

I am so much engaged in making it a reality,

That I oft forget that getting her is just a dream.

15. You

It's vast and deep,
And always true.

Your heart is like a rose,
Fragrant and pure.
Your kindness shines like the sun,
Of that, I am sure.

With every step you take,
You spread love and light.
Your grace and strength inspire,
Through every day and night.

Like the colours of a rainbow,
You bring joy and hope.
You lift us up with your words,
And help us learn to cope.

So, thank you for being you,

For all that you do.

You make the world a better place,

And that is truly true.

16. What Is a Man Without These?

What is a man without hatred?

Gentle

What is a man without pride?

Humble

What is a man without anger?

Serene

What is a man without love?

Just-Alive

What is a man without fame?

Stranger

What is a man without a name?

Useless

What is man without hope?

Dead

17. The Way of Our Love

The way I love you,

Is The way you love me.

And The way we love,

Is no way anybody can.

How much I love you,

Is how much you love me.

And how much we love,

Is no weigh anybody can.

Our love is a force,

That cannot be contained.

It's a powerful connection,

That will never be restrained.

So let's cherish our love,

And hold it dear in our hearts.

For the way we love each other,

Is a love that never departs.

And thank God for,

Love is not a quantity that physically exists.

But only if it would be,

Our hearts would burst out the moment we met.

18. Switch

A lot of them come in and go,

But for you and to you,

Some pray,

Some betray.

The art that is now hard as stone,

Was once a soft piece of clay.

You know,

I know.

You are not today,

The one you were yesterday.

19. BEGINception

Everything's not going to be cosy,

If you are being lazy.

Are you agitated that you are going to muddle around?

Nobody, not even you know your calibre.

What are going to face?

A cliche

Life is too short so,

Start now.

Try to take a first step.

Try to start and then see.

You might be lazy and you might be tired,

But the time isn't.

20. Depleted Nights

No matter what ever I do,

In my dreams,

Your thoughts always seem to be creeping.

All of a sudden in an obscure,

You come in with your smile that illuminates
my heart,

Concurrently your evocations,

Capriciously change my Frame of mind.

For a long time,

You are the only thing for which I have been
seeking.

We are now miles away,

And we have the same night.

But the difference between us is:

You are in a solace,

Spending it sleeping and

I reminiscing us,

Am spending it weeping.

21. Women = Wonder

Their happiness like rain,

Anger like thunder.

Their heart is beautiful like a meadow,

and the mind is kind of straight like a
meander.

Whoever points a finger at them and tells
them to stop,

Is obviously in disguise a blunder.

For a man they are:

A mother, A sister, A wife, A friend,

A daughter and even a grandmother.

But indeed,

they are all women,

And

Undeniably they are a Wonder.

22. The Gaze

Your gaze upon me, so intense,

Draws me in, it makes no sense.

But as I look into your eyes so bright,

I see rejection, with all its might.

Your beauty, it's true, is magnificent to
behold,

But your eyes, they reveal a truth that's bold.

A mirror to your soul, they show,

The pain and hurt that you may know.

So even though I feel the pull of your gaze,

I must respect the truth that it conveys.

For while your beauty is something to admire,

I see the rejection in your eyes, an undeniable
fire.

Perhaps one day you'll see, the beauty that's
within,

And your eyes will show a different spin.

But until then, I'll honour what I see,

And let your rejection set me free.

23. Beauty

Beauty here

Beauty there

Beauty everywhere

But, beauty can you feel?

Mistakes not seen as mistakes

Sins not as sins

Beauty has caused the senses to seal

First excitement

Then curiosity

Then experience

Then pain

beauty causes anyways

And so seldom does it heal.

24. A Grudge Holder

I am envious of the sunlight,

That each morning kisses her face.

Beneath its warm and gentle touch,

Her radiance fills every space.

I am envious of the air,

That caresses her skin with every breeze.

It feels her curves, it holds her shape,

In a way that makes me weak in the knees.

But the air does not see her beauty,

As I do with every passing glance.

It does not see the depth of her soul,

Or how her love can make my heart dance.

Jealous of all these elements,

I pray for the chance to be by her side.

To bask in her glow and feel her warmth,

As our hearts and souls intertwine and collide.

And even as time may take its toll,
And her hair turns grey and wide.
I know she'll still be just as beautiful,
For her inner light will never subside.

25. Definition

I am a human

But I'm more than that.

I am of words

Words - magic.

I am more,

Than all these flesh and bones.

Story - a bit tragic

I am more,

Of soft clay less of stones

I am the book in the upper corner of the shelf

For only the ones who care to read it,

Will truly know who I am.

26. The Joker and The Queen

Come with me,

Hold my hand.

We'll roam around the sea,

And rest ourselves in the sand

Come with me,

Have some faith.

Follow me,

I'll follow your breath.

Come with me,

Keep the books back in those shelves.

We'll sit under the shade of the tree,

And dive into ourselves.

I wonder I could tell you all these things,
You are a queen and I'm a mere joker.

But,

We know often queens fall for kings.

27. Difference

Making love and creating love,
are forms very different.

Although creating love may sound like vanity.

Because making love gives birth,
To something of your inherent.

But,
Creating love indeed propagates Humanity.

28. Stranger Beings

We never want to walk,

But always want to fly.

Just to be validated,

We've normalised telling a lie.

And we always forget,

That our end is nigh

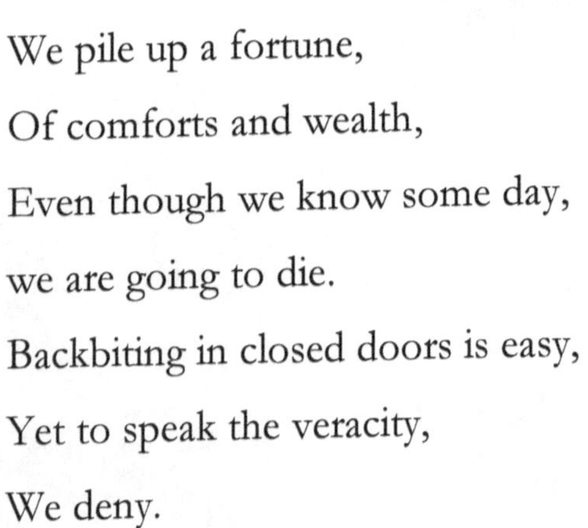

We pile up a fortune,

Of comforts and wealth,

Even though we know some day,

we are going to die.

Backbiting in closed doors is easy,

Yet to speak the veracity,

We deny.

Masculinity questioned,

if a man starts to cry

Femininity questioned,

if a woman isn't shy

All of this but why?

I guess,

This poem barely makes any sense for
humans.

Perhaps,

It is sense

which I am talking about.

Which you don't make any,

and nor do I.

29. The Roads of My Country

Beautiful modest women, and old men half naked,

Unintendedly dark and tan faces of hardworking men like clay baked.

Smiles purest and shimmering eyes with glare,

Friends of unrelated ancestors, hands on the shoulders - the best pair.

Where the language of love is spoken,

Even from the ones the most broken.

Tea is the strength,

A sip of it can lead the men to talks of depth.

Worn and weary with their sturdy sticks,

Children with the school bags and the father
that picks.

Dumb and minds sharpest sheer,

All of it you'll find them here.

                    Hands held by lovers,

         The most wonderful hair with flowers.

                         You never know,

                                    But,

                    People of every kind,

On the roads of my country, you'll find.

30. Similarity

Yes, you fall,

(On Earth)

When gravity of Love pulls you.

Yes, you all,

Shall taste the Death when life kills you.

But in love,

Someone raises you up.

And in death,

Someone buries you beneath.

Neither Love

nor Death

happen expectedly

But both of them give you a new life!

31. Last Night…

Last night,

    I had a dream

        And the dream had me.

           Where I had you,

               And you

had me.

I found a home within you

    Named as we.

      The dream was so nice and
delightful

          But in reality,

             Can it be?

32. Ah, Those Moments!!

I wished those moments would linger and last,

But alas,

They slipped away too fast.

If only I knew magic,

I'd cast a spell to make them vast,

So, they'd endure and not be past.

Yes,

Though fleeting and short,

I yearned for them to be vast.

So, when I grow old,

I'll recount them as stories of my past.

33. Footsteps into Love

Entering the realm.
Sweet essence of roses,
And all those beautiful flowers and butterflies.
Far away from these orchards,

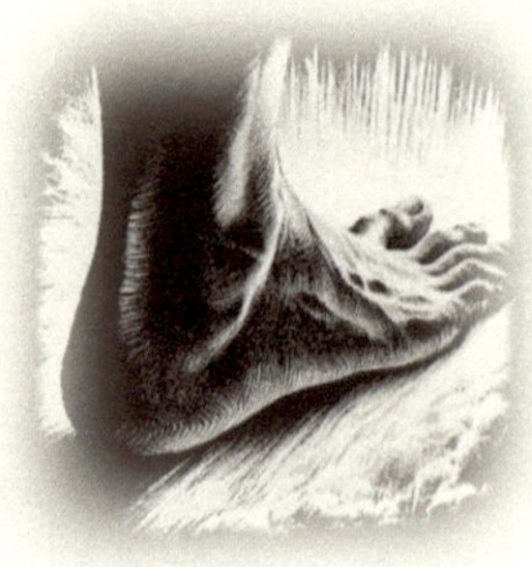

A home.
A decorated door
with a lock.
A mystery to explore,
Only possible way to
open,
A key-
You and I,
Forevermore.

As the door swings open wide,
Sunbeams pierce the darkness from inside.
Fractured walls,
Sorrys and kisses of atonement.
Oh, the hearts confide.

Walking through the narrow hallway,
I fell into the chamber of secrets.
A feeling of dread.

Eyes opened.
Treasures found,
Crates of caresses,
And crates of intimacies,
Chests full of memories and intricacies.
And a secret pathway.
Seemingly unfinished,
Nothing visible through.
Only darkness,
Only stillness,
The essence of mud.

Maybe it's death.

34. My Angel

Mine is not that of your typical type,

She creates a lot of hype,

But in other matters, she may differ,

Not the fairy-tale angel, but one that's
Grander.

No feathers, just skin, her beauty unfurled,

Radiating colours, not just white in this world.

Her eyes guide me with their loving essence,

Always by my side, a constant presence.

She's my angel, a natural spangle,

Not your fairy-tale, but a dream I can
dangle,

Not reality, but a cherished delight,

A vision that graces my nights under
moonlight.

35. A Riddle

The more you get of it,
The more you ask of it.

The more you ask of it,
The less you get of it.

What is it?

Words?

                                        Information?

Grace?

                                                Time?

Knowledge?

                                        Possessions?

Happiness?

                                                Attention?

Success?

Love?

Life?

Everything?

In seeking more, we lose the gain,
Desire's cycle, a puzzling chain.
The more we ask, the less we find,
A riddle of life, a curious kind.

36. Serendipity

A bird here with wings on its eyes,

A beautiful bird from far away appears,

A delightful surprise.

A meeting with no plan,

Set by no man,

Loving seems like an option,

Isn't it something we can?

Butterflies all along,

As the eyes are set from both sides,

Thoughts-

Only love,

Only love,

Only love,

But the shame that divides.

Everything's an imagination.

Life and love,

Love and live,

Wander and lust,

All needs of two strange birds from two strange places.

Only a wish:

And I wish the best

This two birds,

Will they ever share a nest?

37. Echoing solitude

Assertiveness peaks, yet withdrawn by
invisible ghosts.

I've encountered too many souls steeped in
sorrow,

Too many carcasses of grief-stricken hearts,

Encountered Me, myself, and my desolate
essence,

All draped in melancholy.

Fear grips me—

Fear of losing the longing for love,

The zest for life,

The yearning for desire.

These souls shun human company,

Daylight offers respite,

But with the night, loneliness envelops me,

I become the solitary companion,

Gaslit by the eerie silence.

Now, I seek out joyous souls,

Whose crowns gleam with contentment,

Madness or mirth, I care not,

I yearn to meet Me, myself, and my spirit.

The greatest enigma I confront,

Why do they vanish under the moon's gaze?

38. The War within

I've had a war within my head,

A war between the truths I want to write,

And the beautiful lies that everyone else wants
to read.

Some days the war suddenly stops.

Utter peace,

No war has nothing to make me think,

The silence of darkness,

So pretty it seems,

But holds so little glory.

I start to miss the war,

I can't live without it.

The light of chaos,

Is better than the silence of darkness.

I thought the war would kill me,

Nay, it is the silence that will.

Just to give the war a spark,

I slept with a reason.

There I was, more than awake but asleep.

Before that with no war,

I was more than asleep but awake.

I want to sleep,

So that I wake up in the world build by the
people,

Those people who do not know me,

But I'm the world here and everything
happens here with ironies,

The snake eats its own tail,

An hour glass that remains the same volume
but never ends,

The staircase that has the end and beginning
at the same place.

So, there shall be war within me.

I have slowly developed a need for it.

The war gives wisdom of tactics,

Of what's good will win,

And I shall win a heart,

By writing in a state of war within,

Than remaining idle,

In a state of bliss and peace.

I shall write the world,

And the ones with a war going on with
themselves will understand it.

39. Surroundings

I am surrounded with poems,

Beautifully metaphorical and magical.

I am surrounded with songs,

Melodious and audible to the deaf.

I am surrounded with novels,

Vivid and enchanting.

I am surrounded with tales,

Too many yet inspiring.

The surroundings

The poems, the songs, the novels and the
tales and many more wonders,
incomprehensible to my mind.

All,

Complete.

I,

I am started a poem with a rhythm of a song,

Continued as a novel's plot and end with the tale's introduction.

Incomplete in all dimensions,

Nuisance in all languages,

And

Maybe the end will be incomplete.

The surroundings do not understand my existence,

I'm one of them,

But in fragments.

The surroundings do not know how to get me together,

They think,

I'm a whole.

I ask the surroundings,

What am I?

The surroundings say I am [   ].

40. Entropy

This flesh,

These bones,

The veins,

All made up of chaos,

Making patterns like dried up trees.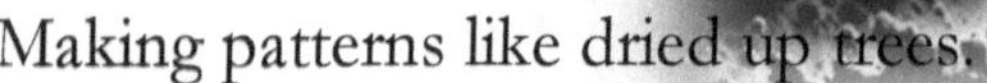

All upon the dust that you call my body.

The dust that doesn't just fall off.

I know I'm made of stars,

Stars are made of dust,

I'm made of dust,

My sublime siblings,

They burn to light up the universe of dust,

I need to burn up too,

To light up the world of dust,

To give liberty from the cold,

To create chaos of order,

To kill the order of chaos,

To become a light bringer,

To become a star,

And to become dust again.

41. Ingratitude

Glass in sand, overlooked the rest.

Gold in mud, led to unrest.

Coal underground, burnt without a sound.

My hatred found, left me alone, unbound.

42. What I know?

I was a whole,

Now, what is a whole?

I was in light,

Now, what is light?

I was with me,

Now, where am I?

I was alive,

Now, what is life?

I know not what I did,

Now, I know what did not already.

Now, I know pieces,

I know darkness,

I know loneliness,

I know the angel of death,

I know a head full of shit that does nothing
but wander alone in the void.

43. Belief

In the silent dance of shadows and sight,

Some blind to events yet grasp their might.

Others feel the echoes before the view,

A realm of hope, comprehension anew.

From a higher power, hope unfolds,

Comprehension's tale, untold thresholds.

I've glimpsed naught, yet I truly know,

Mercy's embrace in the merciful flow.

Adam's repentance, Enoch's unveil,

Abraham's faith, Noah's steadfast sail.

Moses prophesied, Solomon's wisdom
gleamed,

David's position, Mary's patience esteemed.

Jesus' birth, Jacob's unwavering scope,

Joseph's beauty, Job's enduring hope.

Muhammad's character, a beacon so bright,

Guiding through darkness, revealing the light.

Yet, what intrigued me in this cosmic play?

Not the virtuous, but the devil's dark array.

To sway an imbecile to believe and see,

The contrast of darkness, the light within me.

The one who knows God, endless lore,

The one who doesn't, in ignorance's core.

44. No Idea

In those dance of days,

No idea how it was spun.

Once the bringer of light,

Now undone.

Life anchors took it as pride,

For the sons and daughters inside whom it
resides.

The might, the power,

Their vision so clear.

Wisdom and will,

In the right hour so near.

They have no ideas,

Of the ideas they bear.

The youth's power,

Yet no awareness to declare.

In the realm of possibilities, they trail,

'No ideas' echoes the present youth frail.

45. Floods

You say you come alone,

But do you?

You bring forth a tsunami,

A tsunami that floods me with beautiful memories.

To my mind that's not very fertile,

You bring too much,

A beautiful burden,

So I must choose what to remember,

Shall I remember the smiles?,

the laughter?,

the tears wept in wanting?

Shall I remember me?

Or you?

What and who shall I remember?

Maybe, I must write it down.

But I am too lazy for it.

So, To remember everything,

I must persist being in the flood often,

Let me kiss my ocean, Dive in it,

Let me become the ocean,

I've breathed air for too long,

Now I need to breathe love.

Found only in your floods.

I want to hear it,

Your sighs, your heartbeat in dark silences,

I want to feel the warmth of your smile,

Unspoken but true, I'm lonely as an Isle.

These floods of your memories keep me
occupied and content.

Hence, take me away,

Take away this lonely Island,

That's waiting to become the ocean,

And Flood it for eternity.

46. Oops!

I have accidentally started to like my Loner
persona again.

I'm enjoying watching my own shadow,

Rubbing my sweaty hands over the clothes.

No expectations,

Only myself that I crave.

I was Showing parts that weren't mine,

Keeping them hidden again feels brave.

My delusions are fading away,

I can see clearly again.

True company was always myself,

So, I won't be this again,

'Cause I'm keeping the. "Not me" book back
in the shelf.

47. Business

I only buy truths.

Because I know,

All lies aren't sweet and all truths aren't bitter.

Truth must be your USP,

And I will believe in what you utter.

48. Nocturne

As the night stands still,

When I see nothing but darkness covering the sky,

When I hear nothing but melancholy echoing loud,

When I smell nothing but silence burning on the ashes of memories,

When I feel nothing but a part of you,

That remains within me.

Telling me,

"Oh, you are a fool.

That is lost within the realm of nothingness."

And the fading away foolish part of me,

Replying incessantly,

"I agree,

Yes, I am.

But this foolish hopes,

That some night,

The moonlight that I am wishing for,

Will knock at my door."

81

49. A Child that asks

In your presence, I'm not myself, it's true,

An innocent child, I become when I'm with you.

You, the guardian, guiding my way,

As I'm in awe of everything you display.

Like a child before a fridge, seeking a treat,

I reach for your lips, so tender and sweet.

They have the power to calm my racing heart,

You hold the choice to keep us apart or be a loving part.

50. The Boy

There was a boy,

Who was short and skinny with bloated cheeks,

His favourite place,

The school playground.

But only along with his two mates,

A boy with a turban and other with pointy hair,

His pillow was the mother's lap.

So many vehicles he sat on,

But his favourite ride was on his father's back,

As he travelled from one room to another,

He never got bored of it.

He thought he was weird,

And in fact he was.

His place of fight was with his brother,

And then,

The place of unite was with fifty-fifty of the chocolate.

Nowhere did he feel safe,

Except for his mother's arms.

When he had tears in his eyes,

The best support was his father's hand.

His secret treasure was with his two other
weird mates.

There would be two pillows on the bed,

Yet he used to sleep on his brother's tummy,

With his legs on the pillow.

This boy I had seen very closely,

He was strange,

He was weak,

He thought he was stupid,

But he was me.

And where is that boy now?

51. Where is that boy now?

Where is that boy now?

He's in the corners of the ruins of the palace of memories,

Eagerly wanting to come out.

But afraid,

Because he remembers what happened last time.

When he wanted to stay as he was,

But grew up.

He remembers the time,

When he realised everything was not perfect as it seemed.

He loves everyone,

But unlike those times,

He's afraid he won't be loved as he was.

He's afraid that his goodness will be exploited again.

That his kindness will go in vain.

But he's still there,

Waiting,

Some bits of nostalgia bring him back,

But they appear to be fading,

He loves summer and the warm people,

Ironically it is a hard winter now,

And every being is cold.

Be it Hiding or waiting,

I'm at ease,

That he's alive,

But what haunts me is,

For how long will he be alive?

52. Warm

Global warming's just a pun,

Children writing essays for fun.

Unseen yet coldness widespread everywhere,

Children fighting for the proof of who is the rightful heir.

Lifeless and heartless things being created more,

Children of lovely creatures left to die sore

Harder it becomes every day to breathe,

Doctors outnumber the times you and the family meet.

Still here we are faking a smile,

Even though deep down we are lonely as an Isle.

All of these first world problems of yours and mine,

Can fade away and everything will be fine.

Only if we stop complaining and stop finding bugs,

If we get closer to the loved ones and receive the warmest of hugs.

Epilogue

Fear and hope-so beautiful,
Fear darkens the heart with limitations.
Hope lightens it up with purpose.
Everything that is able to kill me,
The air,
The heat,
The water,
The cold,
The people I love,
Myself,
Are the things keeping me alive.
This dance of hope and fear makes us human,
Let us be,
Let others be,
What we were meant to be,
HUMAN.

<u>*Your Perception*</u>